The Book of
CHANGE

The Book of
CHANGE

MAKING LIFE BETTER

Cyndi Haynes

**Andrews McMeel
Publishing**

Kansas City

The Book of Change

For information, write Andrews McMeel Publishing,
an Andrews McMeel Universal company,
4520 Main Street, Kansas City, Missouri 64111.

00 01 02 03 04 RDC 10 9 8 7 6 5 4 3 2 1

Library of Congress Cataloging-in-Publication Data
Haynes, Cyndi.
   The book of change : making life better / Cyndi Haynes.
      p. cm.
   ISBN 0-7407-1006-0 (pbk.)
      1. Change (Psychology) 2. Success—Psychological
aspects. I. Title.
BF637.C4 H39 2000
646.7—dc21   00-035568

Book design by Holly Camerlinck

This book is lovingly dedicated to Andrew.

May you always follow your dreams.

ACKNOWLEDGMENTS

I wish to thank the wonderful people at Andrews McMeel Publishing, especially my editor, Jean Zevnik, for believing in this book. Your hard work and support on my behalf means the world to me!

Dear Reader:

I have always loved the idea of fresh starts and new beginnings. As we turn the pages of history and enter into the new millennium, I can't imagine a better time to make changes in ourselves and in our lives. It is my most sincere wish that you will find within these pages ideas that speak to your heart and the encouragement you need to make your desired changes. May this book open up doors to your personal happiness that you never even dreamed were possible!

Most warmly,

Cyndi Haynes

The Most Popular
Changes People Make:

- Dieting

- Eating healthy

- Saving money

- Getting a new job

- Spending more time with family

- Getting closer to God

- Becoming a better person

- Giving more money to charity

- Volunteering time to community service

- Working fewer hours

- Getting a new look

- Reading more

- Keeping the house tidier

- Stop smoking

- Stop drinking

- Exercising regularly

- Having more romance in one's marriage

- Being a better parent

- Learning a new job skill

- Traveling to exciting places

Today is a new day. You will get out of it just what you put into it. . . . If you have made mistakes, there is always another chance for you. And supposing you have tried and failed again and again, you may have a fresh start any moment you choose, for this thing that we call "failure" is not the falling down, but the staying down.

— MARY PICKFORD

Finish every day and be done with it. You have done what you could. Some blunders and absurdities no doubt crept in; forget them as soon as you can. Tomorrow is a new day; begin it well and serenely and with too high a spirit to be cumbered with old nonsense. This is all that is good and fair. It is too dear, with its hopes and invitations, to waste a moment on yesterdays.

—RALPH WALDO EMERSON

You have to
    stay awake
to make your
    dreams come true.

—Author Unknown

We are always
getting ready to live,
but never living.

—RALPH WALDO EMERSON

The Best Changes
Are:

- Broken down into small steps

- Well planned

- Designed to improve you or your life

- Easy to understand

- Memorable

- Shared with friends and family

- Written out formally

- Heartfelt

- Compatible with your belief system

- Achievable

- Worthwhile

Begin at once
to live,
and count each day
as a separate life.

—LUCIUS ANNAEUS SENECA

There are two things to aim at in life: first to get what you want and after that, to enjoy it. Only the wisest achieve the second.

—LOGAN PEARSALL SMITH

The safest principle
through life,
instead of
 reforming others,
is to set about
perfecting yourself.

— B. R. HOYDEN

The best victory is to conquer self.

—AUTHOR UNKNOWN

We can change
our whole life
and the attitude
of people around us
simply by
changing ourselves.

—Rudolph Dreikurs

The Most Popular Wants and Needs That Call for a Major Change:

- Finding a mate
- Finishing school
- Buying a home
- Getting a new job

A task without
vision is drudgery.
A vision without a
task is a dream.
A task with a vision
is victory.

—AUTHOR UNKNOWN

The mind is the
master of man,
 and so "they" can
who think
they can.

—NIXON WATERMAN

It is in the
changing
that one
finds purpose.

—Hergelitus

To remain young
one must change.

—ALEXANDER CHASE

When you are through changing, you're through.

—BRUCE BARTON

Driving at
one goal
is the
starting point
to another.

—JOHN DEWEY

Nothing happens unless first a dream.

— CARL SANDBURG

Act as if
it were impossible
to fail.

—DOROTHEA BRANDE

The quitter gives the match away

Past all denying;

I think it is better to stay

And fail by trying

—EDGAR A. GUEST

Change is not made without inconvenience, even from better to worse.

—Richard Hooker

Ya gotta do what ya gotta do.

—SYLVESTER STALLONE

Find a
Change Buddy
Who Is:

- Positive

- Supportive

- Dreaming of great things for you

- Available

- Believing your goals are obtainable

- Wanting you to succeed

- Spiritual

- Improving himself

- Up-front with you

- Willing to take you to task when you aren't keeping to your plans

- Enjoyable to work with

- Willing to keep your confidences

Thoughts for Success:

Pray for divine help to make and reach your goals.

Remember that your goals will give you a sense of
direction and purpose, which will help to
make the process of changing a bit easier.

Understand that to be successful in making and
keeping your goals, you must put in the
effort. There are no free rides when it
comes to making changes in oneself or
one's life.

Make sure that your dreams stretch your talents
and imagination.

Create within yourself a deep, heartfelt desire to
change in the direction of your goals,
dreams, and desires.

Keep in mind that the purpose of making changes
is to create a brighter future for you and
your family.

The Most Common Traits of Those Who Set Goals and Attain Them:

- Persevering
- Spiritual
- Bold
- Determined
- Imaginative
- Dauntless
- Plucky
- Creative

- Self-reliant

- Courageous

- Unwavering

- Uncompromising

- Confident

- Brave

It's a funny thing
about life:
If you refuse
to accept anything
but the best,
you often get it.

—W. SOMERSET MAUGHAM

How to Decide on What Changes to Make:

- Brainstorm

- Look for areas of unhappiness

- Look for areas of underachievement

- Get feedback from friends

- Listen to your heart

- Pray

- Ask for advice from loved ones

- Get input from your boss or coworkers

- Ask your child for insights

- Remember your childhood dreams
- Journal your feelings and thoughts
- Experiment with changes

There is nobody
who totally lacks
the courage
to change.

—ROLLO MAY

The Most Common Reasons People Fail to Keep Their Resolutions:

- They aren't completely committed to reaching their goals

- They fail to put them in writing

- They don't make them a priority

- They haven't had success in the past, so they don't make the effort in the present

- They fear success

- They fear change

- They don't want to work hard

- They grow weary along the way

- They fail to remember that change takes time

- They fail to visualize success along the way

I'd rather be
a failure
at something
I enjoy
than to be a success
at something I hate.

—GEORGE BURNS

We should all be
concerned about the
future because we
will have to spend
the rest of
our lives there.

— CHARLES F. KETTERING

If one advances confidently in
the direction of his own
dreams, and endeavors to live
the life which he has imagined,
he will meet with success
unexpected in common hours.

—HENRY DAVID THOREAU

Call Them Changes or Whatever Works Best for You, Like:

- New beginnings
- Fresh starts
- Second chances
- Beginning anew
- Starting over
- Challenges
- Opportunities
- Goals
- Dreams
- Lifelines

Without discipline, there's no life at all.

—KATHARINE HEPBURN

There is only
one corner of the
universe you can be
certain of improving,
and that's your
own self.

—ALDOUS HUXLEY

The Most Common Types of Changes:

- Spiritual

- Financial

- Physical

- Emotional

- Career-related

- Relationship-directed

- Social

- Community

When a man has done all he can do, still there is a mighty, Mysterious agency over which he needs influence to secure success. The only way he can reach it is by prayer.

—RUSSELL H. CONWELL

We change,
whether we like it
or not.

—RALPH WALDO EMERSON

No one
is expected
to achieve
the impossible.

—FRENCH PROVERB

Even if you're on
the right track,
you'll get run over
if you just sit there.

—WILL ROGERS

If you think
you can, you can.
And if you think
you can't,
you're right.

—MARY KAY ASH

The word
impossible
is not in
my dictionary.

—NAPOLEON BONAPARTE

49 The Book of CHANGE

Repeat the Following to Yourself:

- I can

- I will

- I'm determined

- I believe

- I know

Constant effort
and
frequent mistakes
are the
stepping stones
to genius.

—Elbert Hubbard

Success is not
the result of
spontaneous
combustion.
You must first set
yourself on fire.

—FRED SHERO

Winners
never quit
and
quitters
never win.

—VINCE LOMBARDI

Popular Spiritual Changes to Consider:

- Read the entire Bible

- Say grace before every meal

- Count your blessings

- Start a gratitude journal

- Pray each morning

- Pray every night

- Attend church regularly

- Tithe

- Volunteer your time at your house of worship

- Pray on bended knee each day

- Become a missionary

- Teach Sunday school for a year

- Find a spiritual mentor

- Pray throughout your day

- Put God first in your heart and life

- Seek guidance from God about your spiritual changes

- Talk to your religious leaders

The main danger
in this life
are people
who want to
change everything . . .
or nothing.

—LADY ASTOR

The
absurd man
is he
who never
changes.

—AUGUSTE BARTHÉLEMY

When patterns
are broken,
new worlds
emerge.

—TULI KUPFERBERG

You decide what it is you
want to accomplish and then
you lay out your plans to get
there, and then you just do it.
It's pretty straightforward.

— NANCY DITZ

Lost time
is never found.

—BEN FRANKLIN

Be of good cheer. Do not think of today's failures, but of the success that may come tomorrow. You have set yourselves a difficult task, but you will succeed if you persevere; and you will find a joy in overcoming obstacles. Remember, no effort that we make to attain something beautiful is ever lost.

— HELEN KELLER

I think
in terms of
the day's
resolutions,
not the year's.

—HENRY MOORE

Popular Goals
for Singles:

• To date only marriage-potential people

• Make finding a mate a top priority

• Meet a specific number of singles each week

• Create a dating support network

• Be brave and accept blind dates

• Read a dating self-help book every week
or at least once a month

• Try new activities to meet new people

• Be willing to make the first move

• To face rejection in a healthy manner

• Join a new club

- Develop new interests

- Enjoy being single and make the most of it

- Ask dating advice from successful daters

- Learn from past dating disasters

- Stop taking dating so seriously

- Have fun on all dates

- Be realistic

It is a bad plan
that can't
　　be changed.

—PUBLIUS SYERS

One change
always leaves
the way open
for the
establishment
of others.

—NICCOLÒ MACHIAVELLI

Decisions
determine
destiny.

—FREDRICK SPEAKMAN

Choices
   are the hinges
of destiny.

—EDWIN MARKHAM

Happiness
is action.

—DAVID THOMAS

Thoughts for Success:

Keep in mind that if you are looking outside of
yourself for the answers to what changes
need to take place in your life or in your-
self, you need to turn your focus back to
your own heart and soul for the answers.

Teach yourself to love your goals and to view them
as stepping-stones to a new and improved
you.

Understand that behind every change that is
reached is willpower, determination, and
persistence.

Think of your goals as opportunities instead of
viewing them as something difficult.

Put your goals on notecards and place them all
over your:
- Home
- Office
- Car

Create a resolution support network and have
weekly or monthly meetings to encourage
each other.

Find one person who will be your resolution buddy,
whose job it is to encourage you to attain
your goals.

When you write out your goals or resolutions, be
extremely specific.

Ask yourself what is missing from your life and
then compose a list of changes to help you
obtain those missing elements.

If you don't
like something
about yourself,
change it.
If you can't
change it, accept it.

—TED SHACKELFORD

Do what you can,
with what you have,
where you are.

—THEODORE ROOSEVELT

Take time to
deliberate, but when
the time for action
has arrived,
stop thinking
and go in.

—Napoleon Bonaparte

Success is
a matter of luck.
Ask any future.

—EARL WILSON

Tips for Reaching Your Goals:

- Write them down

- Make them a big priority

- Tell others

- Ask for help

- Give yourself a reward for each step that you reach along the way

- Break down big goals

- Try to make this as enjoyable as possible

Every noble work is at first impossible.

—THOMAS CARLYLE

Great works
are performed
    not by strength,
but by
    perseverance.

—SAMUEL JOHNSON

Desire and hope
will push us on
toward
the future.

—MICHEL DE MONTAIGNE

If I don't
get off
the mat,
I'll lose
the fight.

—ARCHIE MOORE

Life is not
simply holding
a good hand.
Life is playing
a bad hand well.

—DANISH SAYING

Most Common Urban Changes:

- Lose weight
- Save/earn more money
- Continue education
- Spend more time with family
- Improve social life
- Slow down hectic lifestyle
- Exercise more

Most Common
Rural Changes:

- Work harder

- Attend church regularly

- Save more money

- Lose weight

- Exercise

- Improve social life

- Spend more time in enjoyable leisure pursuits

Nothing great
was ever
achieved
without
enthusiasm.

—RALPH WALDO EMERSON

Any change,
even a change for
the better, is always
accompanied
by drawbacks
and discomforts.

— ARNOLD BENNETT

What saves a man
is to take a step.
  Then another step.

—ANTOINE DE SAINT-EXUPÉRY

Plodding
wins the race.

—AESOP

No one can
defeat us
unless we first
defeat ourselves.

—DWIGHT D. EISENHOWER

The future is hope.

—JOHN FISKE

Ways to Soothe Your Soul While You Stay True to Your New Change Program:

- Meditate

- Journal your thoughts

- Get plenty of rest

- Eat healthy foods

- Get outside in the fresh air

- Visit scenic spots

- Get in touch with your deepest thoughts

- Lighten up

• Reward your successes

• Don't punish yourself for falling off your program, instead learn from where you went wrong

• Try to make this a fun growing period in your life

The Most Popular Cosmetic Changes:

- Face-lift

- Tummy tuck

- New makeup

- New hairstyle

- New hair color

- Beauty makeover at a spa

- Liposuction

- Chemical peel

- Get an entire new look by having a makeover done by a professional

The hard part
of making good
is that you
have to do it
every day.

—AUTHOR UNKNOWN

The greatest mistake is giving up.

—AUTHOR UNKNOWN

Choose
the best life,
the habit
will make it
pleasant.

—Author Unknown

Change
your thoughts
and you change
your world.

—Norman Vincent Peale

If you
don't know
where you are
going,
you might wind up
someplace else.

—YOGI BERRA

Learn to . . .
be what you are,
   and learn to resign
with a good grace
   all that you are not.

—HENRI FRÉDÉRIC AMIEL

Extra Help for Those Times When You Can't Stick with Your Change Program:

- Start fresh in the morning

- Psych yourself up before beginning again

- Try to understand why you failed
  in the first place

- Take a new approach to reaching your goals

- Call your resolution buddy

- Examine your resolutions to see if they are
  too grandiose

It's the most
unhappy people
   who most
fear change.

—Mignon McLaughlin

Change
is the only evidence
of life.

—Evelyn Waugh

Life
is the sum
of all
your choices.

—ALBERT CAMUS

Great Ways to Help Others Reach Their Goals:

- Applaud the tiniest of successes

- Share your own experiences

- Talk often about their goals

- Support them during difficult times

- Send letters and notes of encouragement

- Buy little gifts as rewards

- Keep track of their record

The Most Popular
Romantic Changes:

- Place your significant other before work, day-to-day responsibilities, and children

- Hug and kiss your significant other every day

- Plan romantic surprises for your mate on a regular basis

- Remember your mate's birthday and all important anniversaries

- Bring flowers and gifts to your mate on a regular basis

- Call your mate when you are going to be late

- Find true love

- Work hard at your love life

- Flirt only with your mate

- Be faithful

- Plan special dates

- Make affectionate gestures on a regular basis

- Try to please your mate

- Be honest with yourself about your love life

- Take care of your own emotional needs

Real adulthood is the result of two qualities: self-discipline and self-reliance. The process of developing them together is the balance called maturing.

—J. W. JEPSON

A certain amount
of opposition is of
great help to a man.
Kites rise against,
not with, the wind.

—JOHN NEAL

Winners do
the seemingly
impossible.

—AUTHOR UNKNOWN

If you can dream it, you can do it.

—Walt Disney

Popular Changes Based on the Time of the Year:

- New Year's Day—all types of goals are set to help create a bright future

- Valentine's Day—to set goals to have a better love life in the future

- Mother's Day—to be a better mom

- Graduation—to make better grades or to complete one's schooling

- June—to become a June bride in the future

- Father's Day—to become a better dad

- July Fourth—to be a better citizen

- Labor Day—to earn more or get a better job
- Thanksgiving—to count one's blessings or to be more spiritual
- Christmas—to keep the true meaning of Christmas alive in your heart all year long
- Birthday—to create a better life or make changes in yourself

It matters not how difficult the task or how many reverses may come, if we keep everlastingly at it and our faith never flags, success will crown our efforts in the end. Faith will move mountains. If headed in the right direction we will reach the goal.

—ARTHUR E. MAYSEY

May you live all the days of your life.

—Jonathan Swift

Don't be afraid
        to take big steps
if one is indicated.
        You can't cross
a chasm in
        two small steps.

—David Lloyd George

The Most Popular Changes in Western Civilizations:

- Dieting

- Personal growth

- Spending more time with family or friends

- Saving money

- Improving overall quality of life

- Finishing school

- Getting a better job

- Attending church regularly

- Having a better love life

- Tithing

Thoughts for Success:

Before getting out of bed and before retiring in the evening, spend five minutes picturing yourself successfully keeping your resolution.

Always write out your resolutions and goals in ink.

Throughout your day vividly imagine yourself reaching your goals.

Create resolutions that are challenging for you, but not unobtainable.

Write out your resolutions on your calendar and on your weekly planner.

Practice positive self-talk regarding your resolutions. Write out statements to use as affirmations.

Share your goals with an "I-told-you-so" type of person to increase your chances of success.

Never stop before success happens!

We must
always change,
renew, rejuvenate
ourselves;
otherwise
we harden.

—JOHANN VON GOETHE

The conscientious plodder is
nearly always outdistanced by
the fellow who stops
occasionally to analyze and
plan.

— W. J. Cameron

Some men succeed
because they
are destined to,
but most men
because they are
determined to.

—Author Unknown

In the long run you hit only
what you aim at. Therefore,
though you should fail
immediately, you had better aim
at something high.

—HENRY DAVID THOREAU

Reward Yourself for Reaching Your Goals By:

- Buying a new outfit

- Eating dessert first

- Buying a piece of fine jewelry

- Going out for a very nice dinner

- Taking a dream vacation

- Playing hooky from work

- Indulging yourself for an entire day

- Rescuing a dog from an animal shelter

- Playing with your child

- Throwing a big party

- Going out for a night on the town

- Preparing your favorite meal

- Sending yourself flowers

- Buying yourself a present

- Ordering something from a mail order catalog

- Sleeping late

- Planning a get-away weekend

Tips for Making Successful Changes:

- Bring a feeling of play and frivolity to them

- Make any necessary changes in a timely manner

- Spend time with people who have achieved what you want to do

- Try different ways to keep your goals fresh

- Listen to your own counsel

Nothing is
so embarrassing as
watching someone
do something
that you said
couldn't be done.

—SAM EWING

Slumps are like
a soft bed.
They're easy
to get into
and hard
to get out of.

—JOHNNY BENCH

Popular Worldwide Goals:

- Political reforms
- Raising the standard of living
- Religious renewal
- Personal growth
- Finding personal happiness

If you wait until the wind and the weather are just right, you will never plant anything and never harvest anything.

—ECCLESIASTES 11:4

Don't wait. The time will never be just right.

—NAPOLEON HILL

Check Your Change History:

- Have you set goals before?

- Were you successful in keeping your resolutions in the past?

- What have you learned in your life about making and keeping your goals?

- Did you have fun with planning and goal setting?

- What helped you to be successful?

- What made it difficult?

- Who helped you to succeed?

- What can you do to increase the chances of your success?

- Did you pray for help?

Very often
a change of self
is needed more
than a change
of scene.

—ARTHUR CHRISTOPHER BENSON

When a
   fight begins
within himself,
   a man's worth
something.

—ROBERT BROWNING

I am the master
of my fate;
I am the captain
of my soul.

—WILLIAM ERNEST HENLEY

Even God
lends a hand
to honest boldness.

—MENANDER

How to Use Affirmations to Keep Your Resolutions:

- Make them present tense

- Be quite specific

- Write them down

- Write them out often

- Say them out loud over and over again

- Post them everywhere

- Sing them

- Make a tape recording of them and listen during your morning routine, drive times, during lunch, and at night

Make
Mini Changes:

• Choose a small area that can use a little boost

• Choose areas that don't require a huge overhaul

• Make changes for a day or a week

• Select a fun, lighthearted area to change

W hen you rise in the
morning, form a resolution to
make the day a happy one for a
fellow creature.

—SYDNEY SMITH

After all, tomorrow is another day.

—MARGARET MITCHELL (SCARLETT O'HARA)

The future comes one day at a time.

—Dean Acheson

Never stop.
One always stops
as soon as
something
is about to happen.

—PETER BROOK

The Most Common Health Changes:

- Eat only healthy foods
- Lose weight
- Get eyes examined/new glasses
- Have a physical
- Have a dental checkup
- Have teeth cleaned
- Floss after every meal
- Brush after every meal
- Wash your hands before eating
- Join a health club
- Reduce stress

- Get a good night's sleep every night
- Drink only in moderation
- Exercise regularly
- Take pet to veterinarian for regular checkups
- Get a flu shot
- Take vitamins
- Take calcium supplements

For everything
you have missed,
you have gained
something else.

—RALPH WALDO EMERSON

The moment
of change
is the
only poem.

—ADRIENNE RICH

The only discipline that lasts is self-discipline.

—BUM PHILLIPS

Know the
true value of time;
snatch, seize
and enjoy
every moment of it.

—Philip Dormer Stanhope

The buck
stops here.

—HARRY S. TRUMAN

Things NOT to Do When Making Changes:

- Be vague

- Put off the starting date

- Forget to write them down

- Listen to the negative voices in your head

- Hang out with resolution-keeping losers

- Wait till New Year's Eve to make them

- Believe that you can't make resolutions throughout the year

- Give up before you reach your goal

Thoughts for Success:

Turn your resolutions into public knowledge. You'll get much more support and interest that way. Plus, it will make you try even harder for you will fear public ridicule if you don't keep them.

Keep at your resolution for at least twenty-one days. It only takes three weeks to turn a new behavior into habit. Keep at it!

Once you decide on a change, write out a list of
five or ten ways that you can reach your
goal. Keep in mind that the more ways that
you have to support yourself, the better off
you will be. Ask your loved ones for ideas.

The Most Common Financial Goals:

• Save at least part of your income

• Pay off all credit card debt

• Stop using credit cards

• Join your company's 401K plan

• Save for retirement

• Save for your child's education

• Learn about stocks

• Learn about investing in bonds

• Hire a financial planner

• Invest in mutual funds

• Learn to live well below your means

- Hunt for ways to save money

- Be thrifty

- Brown bag your lunches

- Buy only on sale

- Ask for discounts

- Only use credit cards that reward their customers

- Pay off your mortgage

Growth begins when we accept our own weakness.

—JOHN VANIER

Readjusting is a
painful process,
   but most of us
need it
      at one time
or another.

—ARTHUR CHRISTOPHER BENSON

Your future depends on many things, but mostly on you.

—FRANK TYGER

I'm going to stop putting things off starting tomorrow.

—SAM LEVENSON

People Who Can Help You to Write Out and Keep Your Goals:

- Spouse

- Mother

- Dad

- Minister

- Coworkers

- Boss

- Roommate

- Best Friend

- Teacher

- Therapist

The Most Popular
Whimsical Changes:

- Travel around the world

- Look years younger

- Become famous

- Make a huge discovery

- Write the great American novel

- Fall madly in love

- Become fabulously wealthy

Thoughts for Success:

Keep in mind that large, important resolutions
require hard work, dedication, and time.

Understand that every little step you take in the direc-
tion of your goal will reinforce the following
steps. It will eventually become easier!

Help yourself and Heaven will help you.

—Jean de La Fontaine

If you aren't
going all the way,
why go at all?

—JOE NAMATH

Make the most
of today.
Translate your
good intentions
into actual deeds.

—GRENVILLE KLEISER

What you are
afraid to do
is a clear indicator
of the next thing
you need to do.

—AUTHOR UNKNOWN

Today is the day in which to express your noblest qualities of mind and heart, to do at least one worthy thing which you have long postponed.

— GRENVILLE KLEISER

Most people put off
until tomorrow
that which they
should have done
yesterday.

—EDGAR W. HOWE

There is no
philosophy
   by which a man
can do a thing
   when he thinks
      he can't.

—AUTHOR UNKNOWN

You must scale
the mountains
if you would view
the plain.

—CHINESE PROVERB

Either do not
attempt at all,
or go through
with it.

—OVID

The Most Popular Community or Social Goals:

- Volunteer time to a worthy cause

- Donate money to a charity

- Help neighbors

- Sign up to be an organ donor

- Give outgrown clothing, toys, and furniture to charity

- Buy what neighborhood children try to sell you

- Be kind to animals

- Work to save the planet

- Vote in all elections

- Take pride in your community
- Tutor underprivileged kids
- Teach someone to read
- Teach English to immigrants
- Pick up litter
- Get all family pets from animal shelters
- Try to end prejudices of all kinds

Thoughts for Success:

Take on new resolutions that come to mind from
the success of reaching your current ones.
Keep stretching yourself. Keep reaching for
the stars.

Remember that you are never too old and you are
never too young to make resolutions.

Make a list of your talents and gifts. Then write
resolutions to enhance them.

Keep in mind that making and keeping your resolu-
tions will often require personal sacrifice.

Create a mid-year checklist and finish it by the last week of June.

MID-YEAR CHECKUP:

- Are you keeping your goals?
- Where have you been successful? Why?
- Where have you failed? Why?
- What can you do to increase your chances of keeping your resolutions?
- What goals do you want to add?

• Do you have any that you want to drop?

• Are you improving because of your changes? How?

• What have you learned along the way?

• Are you helping others to keep their resolutions?

• Are you focused enough?

• Is there a time of day or a specific day of the week during which it is harder for you to keep your changes?

We have no right to give up.
Too many people give up too
early. We are in a stream of
time, and some progress will
take longer; some positive
things will happen after our
lives. If you are really
determined to be on the good
side of life, the forces of the
universe are there to help you.

— ROBERT MULLER

Do your best
every day
and your life
will gradually
expand into
satisfying fullness.

—HORATIO W. DRESSER

Here hath been

dawning another blue day:

think, wilt thou let it slip

useless away.

—THOMAS CARLYLE

If God came in
and said, "I want
you to be happy
for the rest of
your life,"
what would you do?

—BERNIE SIEGEL

Motivation is what
gets you started.
Habit is what keeps
you going.

—Jim Ryun

Habit is stronger
than reason.

—GEORGE SANTAYANA

To learn new habits is everything, for it is to reach the substance of life. Life is but a tissue of habits.

—HENRI FRÉDÉRIC AMIEL

You are younger today than you ever will be again. Make use of it for the sake of tomorrow.

—AUTHOR UNKNOWN

As soon as you open your eyes in the morning, you can square away for a happy and successful day. It's the mood and the purpose at the inceptions of each day that are the most important facts in charting your course for the day. We can always square away for a fresh start, no matter what the past has been.

— GEORGE MATTHEW ADAMS

The Most Popular
Changes for Women:

- Lose weight

- Find true love

- Be a better parent

- Be a better daughter

- Have more time to youeself

- Continue your education

- Get into better shape

- Stop smoking

- Stop buying things that you don't need

- Clean out closets

- Get a totally new look

- Spend time at a spa

- Make your friendships more intimate

- Lighten up

- Have more fun

- Travel

- Find a more fulfilling job

- Become a full-time mother

- Get closer to God

Life wastes itself
while we are
preparing to live.

—RALPH WALDO EMERSON

And if not now,
when?

—THE TALMUD

Vitality shows
not only in the
ability to persist,
but in the ability
to start over.

—F. Scott Fitzgerald

You've got to think about "big things" while you are doing "small things," so that all the "small things" go in the right direction.

— ALVIN TAFFER

All of the
significant battles
are waged
within the self.

—SHELDON KOPP

Change the fabric
of your own soul
and your own
visions,
and you change all.

—Rachel Lindsay

The future
is the past
in preparation.

—PIERRE DAC

There is no failure except in no longer trying. There is no defeat except from within, no really insurmountable barrier save our own inherent weakness of purpose.

— KEN HUBBARD

The Most Popular Changes for Men:

- Career advancement
- Save money
- Be a better parent
- Be a better mate
- Lose weight
- Finish school
- Get into good physical condition
- Invest in stocks and bonds
- Quit smoking
- Eat only healthy foods
- Be a better son

- Travel more
- Cut back on the amount of time spent at the office
- Start your own business
- Get better at sports
- Spend more time with friends
- Have more leisure time

Make a Change Gift Basket for a Friend That Includes:

• Blank book for a resolution journal

• Attractive pen to write with

• Trophy for when your friend has reached his goal

• This book

• Quotes on notecards to place around your friend's home, car, and office to inspire her

• Self-help books

• Candy or other small rewards to celebrate your friend's successes along the way

The Most Popular Changes for People in Their Teens:

- Be drug-free

- Get into the college of your choice

- Make good grades

- Be popular

- Be celibate

The Most Popular Changes for People in Their Twenties:

- Graduate from collage

- Get a good job

- Get married

- Get a place of your own

- Become a parent

The Most Popular Changes for People in Their Thirties:

- Get a big promotion ,
- Build a dream house
- Be a good parent
- Lose weight
- Exercise

The Most Popular Changes for People in Their Forties:

- Save for retirement

- Save for child's education

- Create a healthier lifestyle

- Enjoy life more

- Become a more spiritual person

The Most Popular Changes for People in Their Fifties:

- Eat only healthy foods

- Exercise

- Travel

- Visit with your children and grandchildren more often

- Save for retirement

The Most Popular Changes for People in Their Sixties:

- Start retirement
- Stay healthy and fit
- Travel
- Enjoy life more
- Spend more time with family and friends

The Most Popular Changes for People in Their Seventies and Eighties:

- Stay healthy
- Stay active
- Do volunteer work
- Get closer to God
- Spend more time with family
- Count blessings
- Enjoy each and every minute
- Give financial support to children and grandchildren

- Travel

- Spend time with friends

- Start a hobby

- Read more

Be like a
postage stamp
      and stick to
one thing
until you get there.

—JOSH BILLINGS

To face tomorrow with the thought of using the methods of yesterday is to envision life at a standstill. Even that which we now do well must be done better tomorrow.

—JAMES F. BELL

It is doubtful if anyone ever
made a success of anything
who waited until all the
conditions were "just right"
before starting.

—AUTHOR UNKNOWN

Be wise; begin! He who postpones the hour of living rightly is like the rustic who waits for the river to run out before he crosses.

— AUTHOR UNKNOWN

The Most Popular Changes for Leisure Time:

- Have more free time

- Develop new interests

- Find a hobby that you can share with your mate

- Try a new activity each month

- Travel more

- Spend more time with family

- Spend more time with friends

- Join a new social club

- Spend more time with your pet

This is not a dress rehearsal. This is *it*.

—Tom Cunningham

Now or never was the time.

—LAURENCE STERNE

The Most Popular Children's Resolutions:

- Take better care of the family pet
- Help parents more around the house
- Be kinder to siblings
- Save for college
- Tithe
- Get a good part-time job
- Make better grades
- Volunteer time to a worthy cause
- Spend more time with family
- Call grandparents more often

The will to do,
the soul to dare.

—SIR WALTER SCOTT

Make it a rule of life never to regret and never look back. Regret is an appalling waste of energy: you can't build on it; it's only good for wallowing in.

—KATHERINE MANSFIELD

Nothing splendid has ever

been achieved except by those

who dared believe that

something inside them was

superior to circumstance.

—BRUCE BARTON

If I shoot at the sun, I may hit a star.

—P. T. BARNUM

Mañana is often
the busiest day
of the week.

—SPANISH PROVERB

The Most Popular Resolutions for Married Couples:

- Save for a baby
- Save for a house
- Move to a nicer home
- Spend more time together
- Communicate better
- Remain faithful
- Worship together regularly
- Never go to bed angry with each other
- Support each other's dreams and goals
- Retire early

- Take a second honeymoon

- Move to an exciting locale

- Save for children's education

- Redecorate the house

- Entertain more often

- Have a weekly date night

- Spend more time with the kids

- Start a joint project or hobby

You must do
the things you think
you cannot do.

—ELEANOR ROOSEVELT

Our life
is what
  our thoughts
    make it.

—MARCUS AURELIUS

A hero
is a man
who does
what he can.

—ROMAIN ROLLAND

Seize the hour.

—SOPHOCLES

There is time
for everything.

—Thomas A. Edison

We cannot do
   everything at once,
but we can do
   something at once.

—CALVIN COOLIDGE

The door
of opportunity
won't open
unless you do
some pushing.

—WILL ROGERS

It is a matter of first beginning and then following it through.

—RICHARD L. EVANS

Little by little
does the trick.

— AESOP

The Most Popular Changes Regarding Your Career:

- Find a more fulfilling position
- Start your own business
- Get a raise
- Get a promotion
- Change careers
- Turn a hobby into a career
- Go back to school for more training
- Work fewer hours
- Take part in your company's 401K plan

Keep in mind that you don't have to start all of your resolutions at one time. Concentrate on one for each of the twelve months of the year. Give yourself thirty days to get comfortable with it. Then try an additional resolution while maintaining the previous one.

Changes Related
to Pets:

• Spend more time with furry friends

• Give pet excellent veterinary care

• Be sure that pet gets plenty of exercise

• Buy only safe toys for pet

• Buy toys regularly for pet

• Take pet on outings

• Get your pet a pet, for you know that
animals love being around other creatures,
otherwise they get lonely

• Get pet's teeth checked regularly

• Improve the quality of pet's life

One today
is worth
two tomorrows.

—BEN FRANKLIN

The man who says,
"It can't be done"
is interrupted
by the man
who is doing it.

—AUTHOR UNKNOWN

The only time
you mustn't fail
is the last time
you try.

—CHARLES F. KETTERING

The only joy
   in the world
is to begin.

—CESARE PAVESE

May God . . . let me strive for attainable things.

—PINDAR

Popular Changes Regarding Friendships:

- Remember your friends' birthdays

- Remember your friends' anniversaries

- Spend more time with your friends

- Don't expect perfection from your friends

- Widen your social circle

- Be a true friend

- Be a true friend to yourself

- Keep in mind that to have a friend you must first be a friend

- Treasure all of your friendships

The Most Popular Goals Set by Families:

- Have more meals together

- Treat all family members with respect and kindness

- Attend church together as a family

- Start more family traditions

- Get a family pet/take better care of the family pet

- Keep house tidier

- Share more chores around the house

- Do more favors for one another

- Take family vacations together each year

- Have a weekly family night out together

- Work together for a worthy cause

- Plan more family reunions

- Visit more often with extended family members

- Start a family album

- Start a family gratitude journal

- Pray together

- Communicate better

Great issues
develop from
small beginnings.

—NORMAN VINCENT PEALE

We conquer
by continuing.

—GEORGE MATHESON

If you
stop struggling,
then you stop life.

—HUEY NEWTON

The truth of the matter is that you always know the right thing to do. The hard part is doing it.

—GENERAL NORMAN SCHWARZKOPF

The Most Rewarding Changes for Dealing with the Difficult People in Your Life:

- Forgive them

- Turn them into friends

- Ask them to forgive you

- Vow not to let them upset you any longer

- View them as teachers brought into your life for the sole purpose of helping you to understand love, compassion, and forgiveness

First say to yourself
what you would be,
and then do what
you have to do.

—EPICTETUS

The Most Popular Goals of Homeowners:

- Buy a new home

- Pay off mortgage

- Redecorate

- Put in a pool

- Buy new furniture

- Update the kids' rooms

- Put in a spa

- Landscape

- Hire housekeeping help

- Clean out closets

Start by doing
what's necessary,
then what's possible
and suddenly
you are doing
the impossible.

—St. Francis of Assisi

We create
our fate
every day
we live.

—HENRY MILLER

We all find time
to do
what we really
want to do.

—WILLIAM FEATHER

To be happy, drop the words
"if only" and substitute instead
the words "next time."

—SMILEY BLANTON, M.D.

It's not that "today is the first day of the rest of my life," but that now is all there is of my life.

—HUGH PRATHER

$\mathbf{W}$e must not promise what
we ought not, lest we be called
upon to perform what we
cannot.

— ABRAHAM LINCOLN

Our greatest glory
consists not in
never falling,
but in rising
every time we fall.

—RALPH WALDO EMERSON

The men who try to do
something and fail are infinitely
better than those who try to do
nothing and succeed.

—LLOYD JAMES

Today
is the first day
of the rest
of your life.

—Author Unknown

Arriving at one goal
is the starting point
to another.

—JOHN DEWEY

Self command
is the
main elegance.

—RALPH WALDO EMERSON

Keep doing what you are
doing and you will keep getting
what you're getting. Start
making positive changes.

—AUTHOR UNKNOWN

Tomorrow's life
is too late.
Live today.

—MARTIAL

The Most Popular
Intellectual Goals:

- Join Mensa

- Have IQ tested

- Earn an advanced degree

- Read works of literary importance

- Study new fields of interest

- Create works of brilliance

- Tutor children

- Teach literacy

- Help mankind

He turns
    not back
who is bound
    to a star.

—Leonardo da Vinci

Men must try and try again.

—LAWSON PURDY

There is
no failure
except in
no longer trying.

—ELBERT HUBBARD

Popular Weekly or Monthly Changes:

- Diet
- Put in extra effort at work
- Help with a community-, school-, or church-related project
- Do a good deed
- Have more fun
- Keep the house neater

Inspiration never goes in for long engagements; it demands immediate marriage to action.

— BRANDON FRANCIS

There are
no shortcuts
to any place
worth going.

—BEVERLY SILLS

Practice yourself
in little things,
   and thence proceed
      to greater.

—Epictetus

Victory belongs
to the most
    persevering.

—NAPOLEON BONAPARTE

I'm not there yet,
but I'm closer
than I was
yesterday.

—Author Unknown

No one succeeds
without effort. . . .
Those who succeed
owe their success
to their perseverance.

—ROMANA MAHARSKI

Men do not fail,
they stop trying.

—Elihu Root

Questions to Ask Yourself to Help You Determine What Changes You Need to Make:

- How would your dream life differ from your current life?

- Why are you here on planet Earth?

- Are you happy? Why or why not?

- When you were young, what were your dreams?

- What are your passions?

- What brings a smile to your lips?

- What are your strengths?

- What are your weaknesses?

- Where are you headed if you continue down the path that you are now on?

- Are you proud of yourself?

- What do you want to have happen in your life?

- What must you do to make your dreams come true?

Life belongs
to the living,
    and he who lives
must be prepared
    for changes.

—JOHANN VON GOETHE

Success seems to be
largely a matter
of hanging on
after others
have let go.

—WILLIAM FEATHER

For you and me, today is all we have; tomorrow is a mirage that may never become reality.

—LOUIS L'AMOUR

When I look
at the future,
it's so bright,
it burns my eyes.

—Oprah Winfrey

Before
you can score
you must first
have a goal.

— GREEK PROVERB

The Most Popular
Moral Changes:

• You will always be truthful

• You will be faithful to your mate

• You will set a positive example for your children

• You will strive to be a person of high
moral character

• You will serve mankind

• You will look out for those less fortunate

• You will try to please God at all times

• You will live the life of a hero

• You will be kind to animals

• You will work hard to preserve the land

- You will take pride in your country
- You will keep in mind that one person's life can make a huge difference in this world
- You will abide by the Ten Commandments

Put your heart and soul into making changes and achieving your goals!

We should every night call

ourselves to an account:

What infirmity have I

mastered today?

What passions opposed?

What temptation resisted?

What virtue acquired?

—SENECA

List of Positive Changes to Consider:

- Become more spiritual

- Create more leisure time

- Laugh more often

- Refuse to be defeated by problems

- Worry less

- Travel more

- Give more of yourself

- Find your true self

- Adopt a pet from a shelter

- Read more

- Watch television less

- Spend more time with loved ones

- Realize the brevity of life

- Lighten up

- Take care of your health

- Count your blessings at the end of each
and every day

- Treasure your children and your parents

- Create a lifelong love affair with your spouse

There isn't a person anywhere who isn't capable of doing more than he thinks he can.

—HENRY FORD

To improve
is to change;
To be perfect
is to change often.

—WINSTON CHURCHILL

What you are
is God's gift to you;
What you make of it
is your gift to God.

—ANTHONY DALLA VILLA

Self-respect
is the fruit
of self-discipline.

—ABRAHAM HESCHEL

Be patient.
You'll know when
it is time for you
to wake up
and move ahead.

—RAM DASS

It is never too late
to be
what you might
have been.

—George Eliot

The indispensable first step to getting the things you want out of life is this: Decide what you want.

— BEN STEIN

Try, try again.

—WILLIAM EDWARD HICKSON

Our greatest
weakness lies in
giving up.
The most certain
way to succeed
is always to try
just one more time.

—THOMAS EDISON

It's never
too late—
in fiction
or in life—
to revise.

—Nancy Thayer

Write out the top ten things you want to change the most in your life.

1.

2.

3.

4.

5.

6.

7.

8.

9.

10.

Write out your top ten goals
for the next week.

1.

2.

3.

4.

5.

6.

7.

8.

9.

10.

Write out your top ten goals for the next month.

1.

2.

3.

4.

5.

6.

7.

8.

9.

10.

Write out your top ten goals
for the next six months.

1.

2.

3.

4.

5.

6.

7.

8.

9.

10.

Write out your top ten goals
for the next year.

1.

2.

3.

4.

5.

6.

7.

8.

9.

10.

Once you decide on a resolution, write out a list of five or more ways you can help yourself to reach your goal. Write your list below and keep in mind that the more ways you have to support yourself, the better off you will be.

1.

2.

3.

4.

5.

6.

7.

8.

9.

10.

Once you decide on a resolution, write out a list of five or more ways you can help yourself to reach your goal. Write your list below and keep in mind that the more ways you have to support yourself, the better off you will be.

1.

2.

3.

4.

5.

6.

7.

8.

9.

10.

Once you decide on a resolution, write out a list of five or more ways you can help yourself to reach your goal. Write your list below and keep in mind that the more ways you have to support yourself, the better off you will be.

1.

2.

3.

4.

5.

6.

7.

8.

9.

10.

Once you decide on a resolution, write out a list of five or more ways you can help yourself to reach your goal. Write your list below and keep in mind that the more ways you have to support yourself, the better off you will be.

1.

2.

3.

4.

5.

6.

7.

8.

9.

10.

Once you decide on a resolution, write out a list of five or more ways you can help yourself to reach your goal. Write your list below and keep in mind that the more ways you have to support yourself, the better off you will be.

1.

2.

3.

4.

5.

6.

7.

8.

9.

10.

Brainstorming/Notes

1.

2.

3.

4.

5.

6.

7.

8.

9.

10.

Brainstorming/Notes

1.

2.

3.

4.

5.

6.

7.

8.

9.

10.

Brainstorming/Notes

1.

2.

3.

4.

5.

6.

7.

8.

9.

10.

Brainstorming/Notes

1.

2.

3.

4.

5.

6.

7.

8.

9.

10.

Brainstorming/Notes

1.

2.

3.

4.

5.

6.

7.

8.

9.

10.

Brainstorming/Notes

1.

2.

3.

4.

5.

6.

7.

8.

9.

10.

ABOUT THE AUTHOR

Cyndi Haynes is a best-selling author of seven books in the 2,002 series, including *2,002 Ways to Show Your Kids You Love Them* and *2,002 Ways to Cheer Yourself Up*. Her books have been published in twelve languages. To promote her books she has appeared on hundreds of radio and television programs, including *Ricki Lake* and *Gordon Elliott*. Her books have been written about in numerous publications, including *Glamour, Redbook,* and *Cosmopolitan*. She lives in Indiana with her husband, son, two golden retrievers, and a Bernese mountain dog.